LOS ANGELES

TOMORROW YOU'LL BE ONE OF US

SCI FI POEMS

CHUCK ROSENTHAL
& GAIL WRONSKY

ILLUSTRATIONS

GRONK

LOS ANGELES

Copyright © 2013 by Chuck Rosenthal, Gail Wronsky and Gronk. All rights reserved. Published in the United States by What Books Press, the imprint of the Glass Table Collective, Los Angeles.

Publisher's Cataloging-In-Publication Data

Rosenthal, Chuck, 1951-

   Tomorrow you'll be one of us : sci fi poems / Chuck Rosenthal & Gail Wronsky ; illustrations, Gronk.

   p. : col. ill. ; cm.

   ISBN: 978-0-9889248-0-2

   1. Science fiction films--Poetry. 2. Mexican American art. 3. American poetry--21st century. 4. Experimental poetry, American. I. Wronsky, Gail Friemuth. II. Gronk, 1954- III. Title.

PS3568.O8368 T66 2013

811/.6

What Books Press
10401 Venice Boulevard, no. 437
Los Angeles, California 90034

WHATBOOKSPRESS.COM

Cover art: Gronk, *Untitled*, 2012
Book design by Ashlee Goodwin, Fleuron Press

TOMORROW YOU'LL BE ONE OF US

CONTENTS

Once my air is out, water won't matter	15
Every woman in the world, we all live in fear	17
Power, power you can't conceive	19
Making a decision like that would scare anyone	21
There's not a drop of booze left in this house	23
Then out of the sky came a solution	25
Red alert—small farm on the coast	27
A spaceship from where? From outer space	29
How's the music of the spheres today?	31
I always dreamed of meeting a young man	33
My evil self is at the door and I have no power to stop it	35
How can you just stand there as if nothing were wrong?	37
A parallel universe with a door	39
Who am I to stand in the way of science?	41
It's a long story but I'll make it brief	43
We're not really going to conquer your world, we're simply saving it from itself	45
I don't want to be around when they find out we're gone	47
It's no use, he knows it's your other self	49
He kept it a secret from everyone, even me	51
Would you look at that moon?	53
It says here, in Spanish of course, "the wells of life"	55
Nobody knows Beth, not even the military	57
The birds will be out of the house by now anyway	59
And so it appears that these beings from another world have appealed for our help	61

Who'd do a thing like that?	63
Slaves do not speak without permission in the presence of the Master of the Moon	65
I keep wondering what she's thinking	67
Something smells like burnt feathers	69
We can't protect you, we can only warn you	71
Something has happened here that isn't in the book	73
I've had enough news for one day	75
Look, friend, you're the prisoner	77
For me, it's not so much a landmark as a journey's end	79
I saw something	81
Two more meteors!	83
Here's to the success of the expedition	85
Soft skin inside his mouth	87
We can't touch it while it's still underwater	89
This is Intervision calling the world	91
Like a dream in the night their civilization perishes	93
I can't get the iceberg out of him!	95
Johnson? Johnson? Johnson!	97
It started with an all-out war between the sexes	99
You have brought death upon all in this room	101
This is where either we die or it dies	103
Here we go again	105
They've classified the sky top secret now	107
You're asking me to sabotage the entire world	109
The tricks they tried, how childish they were	111
If you wish, call it a premonition	113
Her mind refuses to remember	115
Maybe if I call them they will answer—their ghosts will answer	117
A soothing ointment?	119
We would greet them as equal partners in the universe	121
What makes you think Betty's in the cellar?	123
Nothing can resist this power	125

It could be our baby	127
They looked like dead fish	129
Why is it always so costly for man to move from the present to the future?	131
Put the gun away	133
Where would be safer than City Hall?	135
Nothing was effective against them	137
I know, you want to know where you are	139
Tonight for the first time in history a robot killed a man	141
Zontar is on its way, darling	143
After that they started acting strangely	145
Remember what you learned here today	147
It must be a terrible thing to be so afraid	149
Something went wrong, it's as simple as that	151
His mind doesn't want to remember the details	153
Everything *seems* all right	155
Alpha 2 does not answer	157
I present you with the possibility of saving the human race	159
We can't hand out blood like gasoline	161
Coda	163
List of movie titles	165
Acknowledgments	167

FOREWORD

ONE COULD ARGUE that the merits of found poetry often depend upon the source text. Erasures and recalibrations of science journals, literary masterpieces, or the circuitous mumblings of a former Secretary of Defense may exemplify the extent and worth of the artistic license. Nevertheless, Gail Wronsky and Chuck Rosenthal have created here a series of found poems that have as their source material selected bits of dialogue from cultish science-fiction films from the 1950's and 1960's.

Where do B-Movies go to die? In this series, they become poems, composites of otherwise unconnected dialogue that form a larger and mysterious ontology of wonder and hilarity. Take the quirky "A space ship from where? From outer space":

> Handle it gently. It has to get us home.
> You know there have been rumors.
> But what would they want with little Cathy Wilson?
> As an old man I feel free to accept beauty without apology.
> Both of them blown to bits. Any more orders?

This mash-up of tonal dexterity also provides readers with a flash-narrative where the necessary pieces fall into place. The title gives us a peek into the fun in the collaborator's project by showing the profound lunacy and illogic of the source material. What the hell kind of question is "A spaceship from where?" and where else would a space ship come from, if not outer space? I see Leonard Nimoy grabbing his temples and shouting "This shit isn't logical!"

In this poem, as in this series, however, the narrative moves in a short, chaotic pace, making for all the fun in these works. Lines one and two provide a kind of hook to the story. Homecoming, a theme as old as the written word, combines with the threat of scandal. Suddenly, poor little Cathy Wilson is thrown into the mix, and we sense the development of a futuristic *Lolita* narrative about to take place in the cosmos. This, of course, is coupled with the serene concession made by the old man; his acceptance of "beauty without apology" is an adage for the artist. The final line is the appropriate undoing of all parties involved—the sparagmos of the twentieth century. Instead of Maenads ripping Orpheus to pieces for his acceptance of beauty without apology, apocalypse is always lurking under and about the surface of these films. What is the apocalypse but the obliteration of everyone—our *total* sparagmos? While it is easy to scoff at the campiness of these films, therein resides a popular "camp," a grave moral seriousness that serves as the poetic impetus. Wronsky and Rosenthal appear quite aware of this impetus: like the singing head of Orpheus, these fresh and inventive poems emerge from what has been torn apart.

—Cody Todd

Reprinted with permission from the editors of *The Offending Adam*

What a wonderful specimen to have in the museum.

ONCE MY AIR IS OUT, WATER WON'T MATTER

It looks molten. But how does that figure?

What a wonderful specimen to have in the museum.

Have you decoded any other messages?

In one moment we may be able to leap 2000 years.

This is going to be the longest 6 ½ minutes I've ever spent.

Up here on Mars, you've gotta face the reality of being alone forever.

EVERY WOMAN IN THE WORLD, WE ALL LIVE IN FEAR

Up here on Mars, you've gotta face the reality of being alone forever.

Like a jellyfish it was, except it had a kind of shine to it.

I knew these creatures were alive somewhere.

We can tell them this: whatever it is will rise up to the surface and get back at us.

He'll be drunk as a lord.

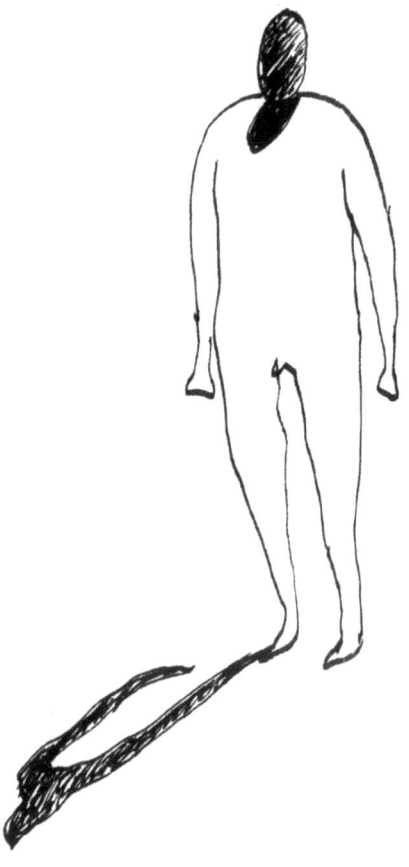

Sometimes I almost want to leave.

POWER, POWER
YOU CAN'T CONCEIVE

And everything living was destroyed by an incredible catastrophe.

Now which way do we go?

This is a key moment in the history of the world.

Where are we going to find trees down here?

It's all right, Sandy. Something will come and save us.

Sometimes I almost want to leave.

You're mad, Stevens. You want to play God.

MAKING A DECISION LIKE THAT WOULD SCARE ANYONE

You're mad, Stevens. You want to play God.

What do you mean conventional explosives are useless?

We've sighted a moving object underneath the water.

And it proves that all the scotch whiskey has not been

exported to America.

May I take your coat?

Mars seems to have run out of messages for the moment.

THERE'S NOT A DROP OF BOOZE LEFT IN THIS HOUSE

Switch out the lights, will you, darling?

Mars seems to have run out of messages for the moment.

We've got to find some heavier stuff.

What are these gizmos? I found them near the corpse.

And I thought you couldn't see with your gloves on.

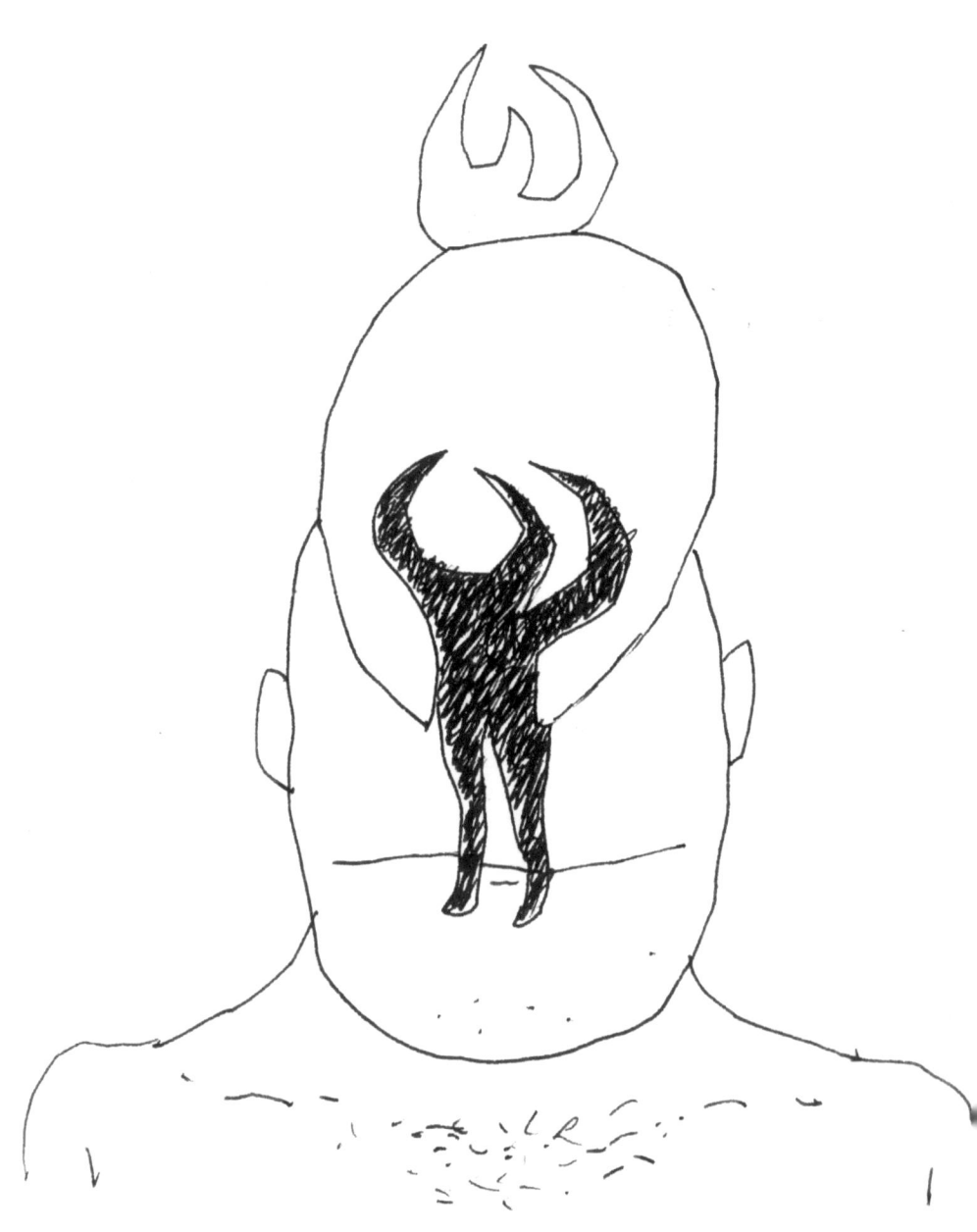

There's no way of telling whether a man is a monster or not.

THEN OUT OF THE SKY CAME A SOLUTION

We can proceed with the next part of our plan.

Just thinking about it is a nightmare.

It really shouldn't be the responsibility of robots.

There's no way of telling whether a man is a monster or not.

I can hate, and I can kill. I'm a man.

Who am I to stand in the way of science?

RED ALERT—SMALL FARM ON THE COAST

It's headed for the beach.

Who am I to stand in the way of science?

There's no stopping the disease. It's out of control.

Then there's really nothing exciting about this at all.

Why did you come? To be kind?

Both of them blown to bits. Any more orders?

A SPACESHIP FROM WHERE? FROM OUTER SPACE

Handle it gently. It has to get us home.

You know there have been rumors.

But what would they want with little Cathy Wilson?

As an old man I feel free to accept beauty without apology.

Both of them blown to bits. Any more orders?

The Martians have got to be using hypnosis.

HOW'S THE MUSIC OF THE SPHERES TODAY?

Mind sharing your table with a couple of strange astronauts?

The Martians have got to be using hypnosis.

At least now we know what our adversary looks like.

A crew of men and women who have one single purpose: to see that

I face a firing squad.

When was the last time you took a pretty girl for a walk?

I'll have less dreaming aboard this ship!

I ALWAYS DREAMED OF MEETING A YOUNG MAN

Flying saucers? Disappearing scientists? What next?

I'll have less dreaming aboard this ship!

What are they doing up there?

You sent your sacred id out to murder them.

I'm not that harmless.

Then how about many giant reptiles?

MY EVIL SELF IS AT THE DOOR AND I HAVE NO POWER TO STOP IT

Will you come in? Over.

For the past two hours I've been anticipating you making that asinine statement.

I'm not trying to play Russian roulette, Bill.

I'm the guy with all the answers.

Id, id, id, id, id.

Don't talk nonsense, Mary.

Then how about many giant reptiles?

Wait a minute. I ain't half finished.

HOW CAN YOU JUST STAND THERE AS IF NOTHING WERE WRONG?

Let us concentrate on this material object.

I'd like to see one of the injectapods.

I shall drain your minds, and bend your wills to mine.

Did your daughter and her boyfriend ever swim here?

Wait a minute. I ain't half finished.

It lies in a tank in that room.

A PARALLEL UNIVERSE WITH A DOOR

It lies in a tank in that room.

How can that thing have gotten aboard?

I have an officially recorded IQ of 183.

And there's no more of it in the dispensary.

This is the only door.

The world is full of lunatics.

WHO AM I TO STAND IN THE WAY OF SCIENCE?

How would you feel if a crazy guy in a helmet with pipes sticking out of it came at you in the dark?

Your guess is as good as mine.

In any case, the question is totally without merit.

The world is full of lunatics.

Now they reflect light like mirrors.

I'd say it sounded like an ultimatum.

You might have chosen a better place to land.

IT'S A LONG STORY
BUT I'LL MAKE IT BRIEF

You might have chosen a better place to land.
Has anyone of you seen anything alive?
What are these gizmos? I found them near the corpse.
Let's not start that flying saucer nonsense again.

Has any of you seen anything alive?
Four flat tires. That's that.
Let's not start that flying saucer nonsense again.
You're saying these Martians could be mutants?

Four flat tires. That's that.
No, we don't think it was a plane.
You're saying these Martians could be mutants?
I don't know. This ain't my neighborhood.

No, we don't think it was a plane.
What was that? Where are the others?
I don't know. This ain't my neighborhood.
Conquest and occupation of the earth will present no difficulty.

What was that? Where are the others?
What are these gizmos? I found them near the corpse.
Conquest and occupation of the earth will present no difficulty.
You might have chosen a better place to land.

A brain is a pretty powerful weapon if you use it right.

WE'RE NOT REALLY GOING TO CONQUER YOUR WORLD, WE'RE SIMPLY SAVING IT FROM ITSELF

I'll take it from here, Bob.

And then I'll have to put more guards on the guards.

A brain is a pretty powerful weapon if you use it right.

I never thought about it—painting as hypnosis.

I don't want to be around when they find out we're gone.

I DON'T WANT TO BE AROUND WHEN THEY FIND OUT WE'RE GONE

We thought you were hurt and wouldn't be able to accompany us on our voyage to the black void of space.

What would Space Commander Connors do in a situation like this?

He'd say that red flare is a pink elephant.

Get the Polaroid.

Invaders of my universe, you are doomed.

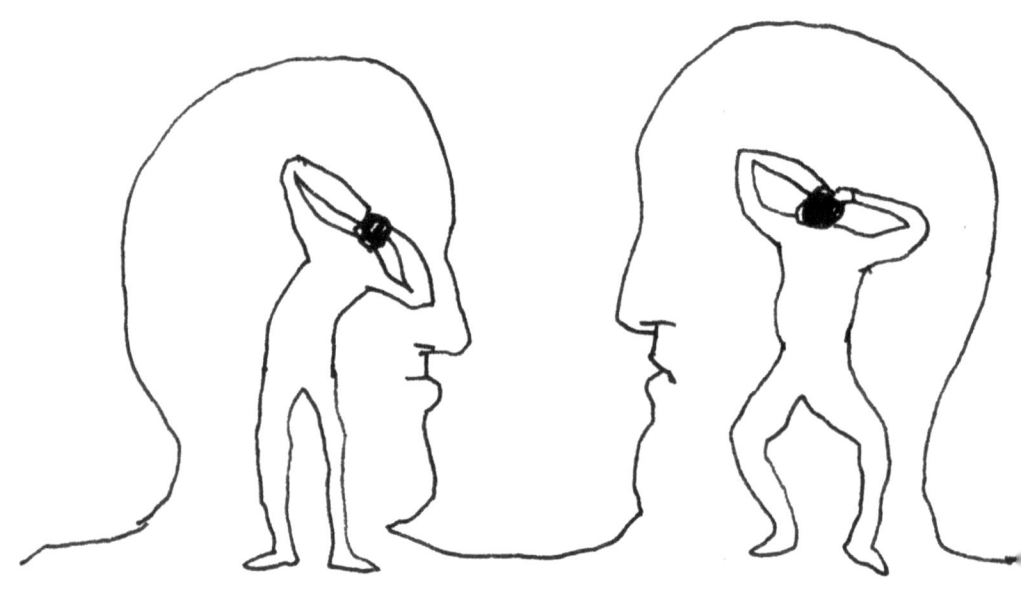

It's no use, he knows it's your other self.

IT'S NO USE, HE KNOWS IT'S YOUR OTHER SELF

Looks like you rushed me here for nothing.

I didn't realize I was being mesmerized.

What good will that do? How can you expect to survive any better than me?

All right, but it's every man for himself.

I'd still like to be there as an observer.

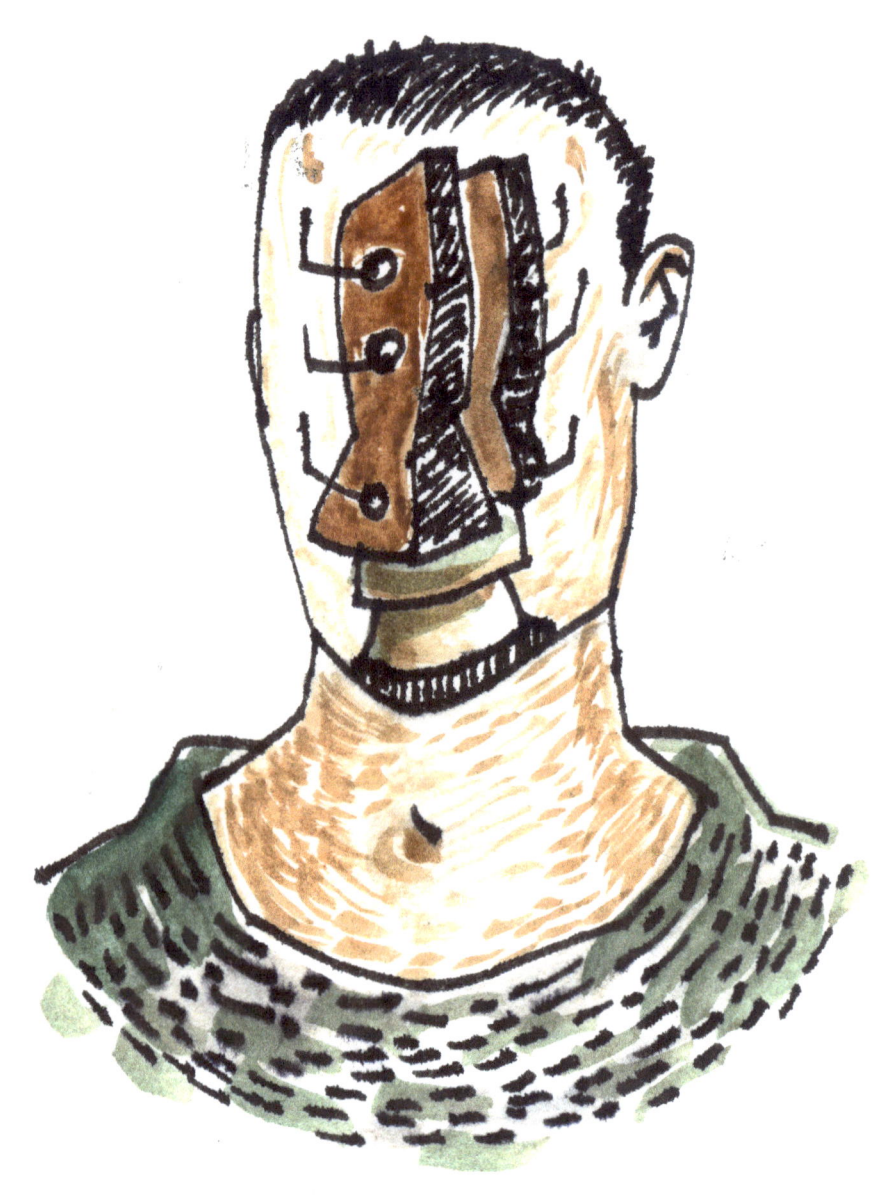

You've had a big dose of x-rays.

HE KEPT IT A SECRET FROM EVERYONE, EVEN ME

Karen, you go with her. I've got work to do.

She appears to have a very high chlorophyll content.

All you did was scratch her and she bled to death.

How do you explain that stuff about the missing head?

You've had a big dose of x-rays.

Would you look at that moon?

WOULD YOU LOOK AT THAT MOON?

Those suitcases must have been loaded with nitroglycerin.

Could use a little paprika.

Commander, there's something surfacing on the port side.

You're twice as heavy as you were on Mars.

How do I know? I can't even spell it.

How can you possibly capture a thing you can't even see?

IT SAYS HERE, IN SPANISH OF COURSE, "THE WELLS OF LIFE"

How long do you expect me to continue this hell?

The long Venutian night is always preceded by a violent storm.

You know, I'm very fond of plants.

I wouldn't mind being conquered by someone like you.

How can you possibly capture a thing you can't even see?

Hey, those trees look different.

NOBODY KNOWS BETH, NOT EVEN THE MILITARY

Hey, those trees look different.

It's impossible! It's insane!

You saved my life. Don't that mean nothing?

So why are you carrying your gun?

I think he remembered he lost his soul.

That's pretty far out. Hope this doesn't take all night.

It's coming after us—look!

THE BIRDS WILL BE OUT OF THE HOUSE BY NOW ANYWAY

You must let me send you a less-monotonous diet.

We can't speed up science, Gruder.

It's coming after us—look!

Now you'll have to face the consequences.

We could dance if there wasn't so much blood around.

All these plants are nothing but men.

AND SO IT APPEARS THAT THESE BEINGS FROM ANOTHER WORLD HAVE APPEALED FOR OUR HELP

It is time, Earthman.
I think we better knock her out.
All these plants are nothing but men.
Perhaps in a way we're being controlled too.

I think we better knock her out.
Not until she has to take some notes for us.
Perhaps in a way we're being controlled too.
Release him, or I'll destroy your leader.

Not until she has to take some notes for us.
Young lady, you are not to discuss that with anyone.
Release him or I'll destroy your leader.
Where did the eagle come from? Why do men have souls?

Young lady, you are not to discuss that with anyone.
I'll take you dancing on Mars. How about that?
Where did the eagle come from? Why do men have souls?
Be ready to get out of here in a hurry.

I'll take you dancing on Mars. How about that?
All these plants are nothing but men.
Be ready to get out of here in a hurry.
It is time, Earthman.

I think you're getting much too involved with these humans.

WHO'D DO A THING LIKE THAT?

I forget the scientific distances that separate us.

Some day you may thank me for that.

What's wrong with killing a snake?

Enough to blow this thing back to Mars.

I think you're getting much too involved with these humans.

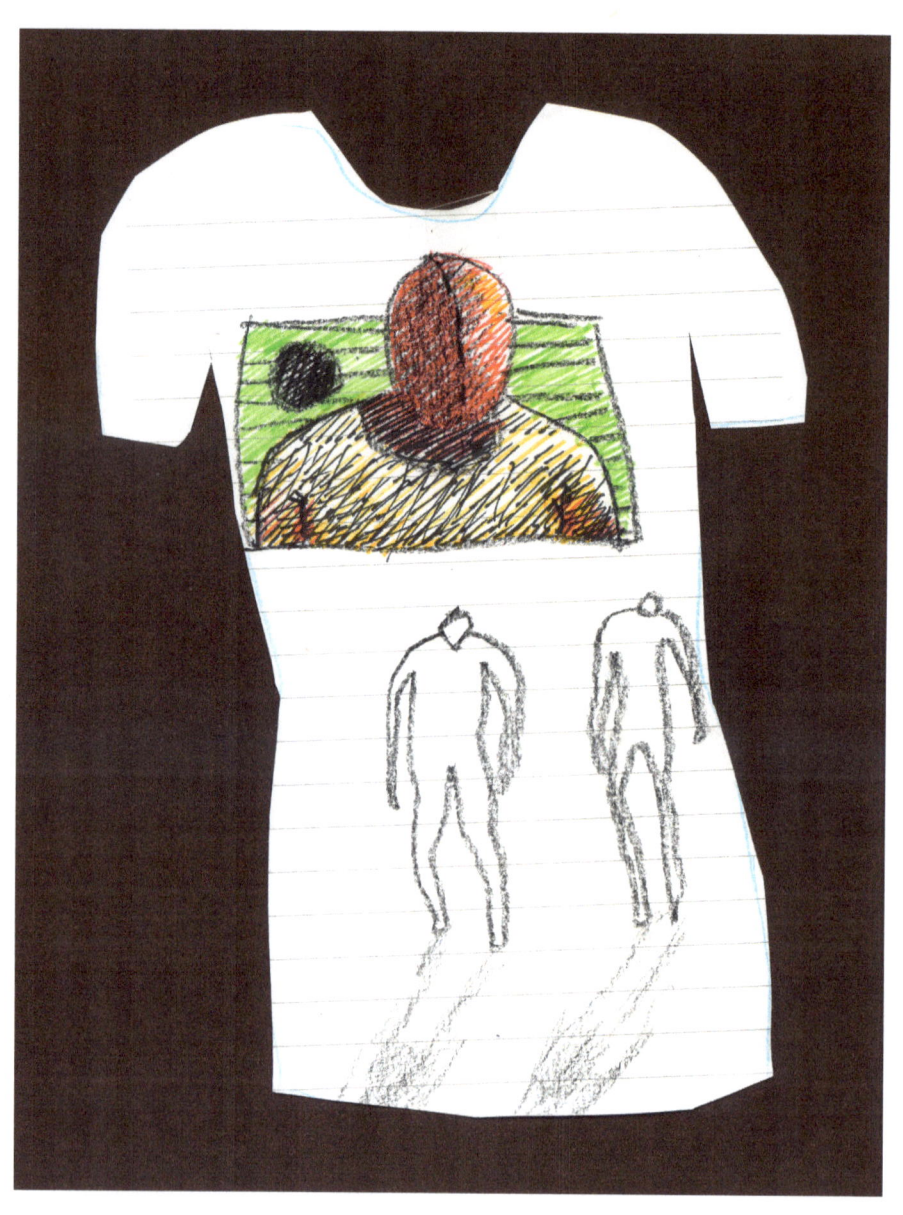

What happened down there?

SLAVES DO NOT SPEAK WITHOUT PERMISSION IN THE PRESENCE OF THE MASTER OF THE MOON

Who are you?

How do I know? I can't even spell it.

What happened down there?

How do I know? I can't even spell it.

Has any of you seen anything alive?

How do I know? I can't even spell it.

Where are you taking me?

How do I know? I can't even spell it.

Do you believe that?

I don't know. Everything is so strange.

I keep wondering what she's thinking.

I KEEP WONDERING WHAT SHE'S THINKING

I've just seen a monster. They look like us—they look just like us.

It can't be Sputnik—it's not listed in the TV Guide.

Either way we all die.

All the more reason to get Jim out of that pit.

I pray that I AM insane.

SOMETHING SMELLS LIKE BURNT FEATHERS

I pray that I AM insane.

I'll take her topside, Colonel.

You say there were no witnesses?

We will transmit again. From Mars.

Sometimes the only way I know you're alive is when I hear you flush the toilet.

I want to go to the moon.

WE CAN'T PROTECT YOU, WE CAN ONLY WARN YOU

The creatures have taken over his body.

It's as if the wind were blowing radioactivity in, then out, then in, then out.

Do you suppose there could be some sort of trap door out there?

Make for the rock.

I want to go to the moon.

*It's like having a grandstand seat for the creation of the world—
or its death.*

SOMETHING HAS HAPPENED HERE THAT ISN'T IN THE BOOK

It's like having a grandstand seat for the creation of the world—or its death.

They looked like dead fish.

Gentlemen, we are witnessing a biological chain reaction.

But I'm going to stay alive, believe me.

What's the matter? No scientific curiosity?

Mars is burning up.

I'VE HAD ENOUGH NEWS FOR ONE DAY

Mars is burning up.

Your destiny is to die.

Shall we keep going?

Look, friend, you're the prisoner.

LOOK, FRIEND,
YOU'RE THE PRISONER

I think I know how to start the reverse process.

What's this dust coming?

He's a scientist, darling. You know it's his duty.

Do you know what I think? That thing up there,

it's a flying coffin.

For me, it's not so much a landmark as a journey's end.

FOR ME, IT'S NOT SO MUCH A LANDMARK AS A JOURNEY'S END

Keep your eyes wide and blank.

Like a bunch of ghosts waiting for a corpse to rot in.

It's your torn suit. Infection is getting through.

Why are you telling me all this?

Why do we have to talk?

Our planet's on fire below us.

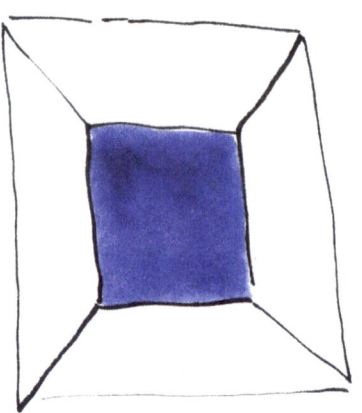

No fire, no smoke, no smell, no sound, nothing.

I SAW SOMETHING

I saw something, like luminous globes, out of the corner of my eye.
Soon my spaceship lands on earth.
It's like a nightmare of unending silence.

The street's deserted, the inhabitants behind their doors.
The sphere is turning red.
I saw something, like luminous globes, out of the corner of my eye.

If only I could be certain of what you're saying.
Now it's got you under its control.
It's like a nightmare of unending silence.

But he was trying to tell us something.
No fire, no smoke, no smell, no sound, nothing.
I saw something, like luminous globes, out of the corner of my eye.

How can you possibly capture a thing you can't even see?
Perhaps in a way we're being controlled too.
It's like a nightmare of unending silence.

It's time to go outside.
We were all wrong.
I saw something, like luminous globes, out of the corner of my eye.
It's a nightmare of unending silence.

Just consider me a piece of furniture.

TWO MORE METEORS!

So who's got time to listen to the radio.

Are you still going under the monster theory?

Don't make it sound threatening.

That's what we have to find out before they kill us all.

Just consider me a piece of furniture.

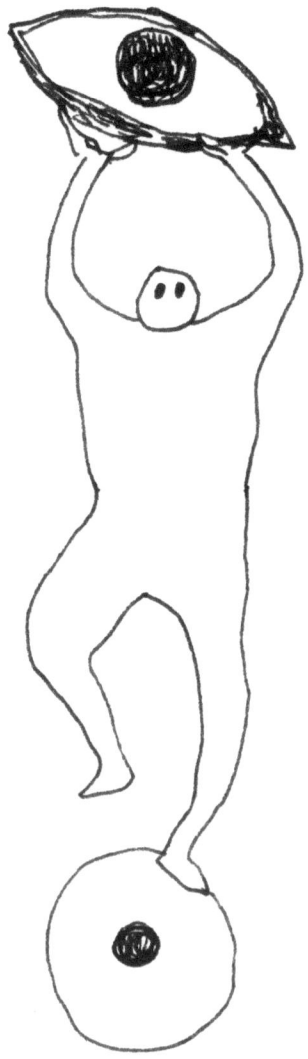

No one on earth has seen such a sight.

HERE'S TO THE SUCCESS OF THE EXPEDITION

I found you on the road, unconscious.

No one on earth has seen such a sight.

It's supernatural—that's what we think it is.

I'm afraid the nightmare has just begun.

That's what's buggin me out of my skull.

Just like he said, all aglow.

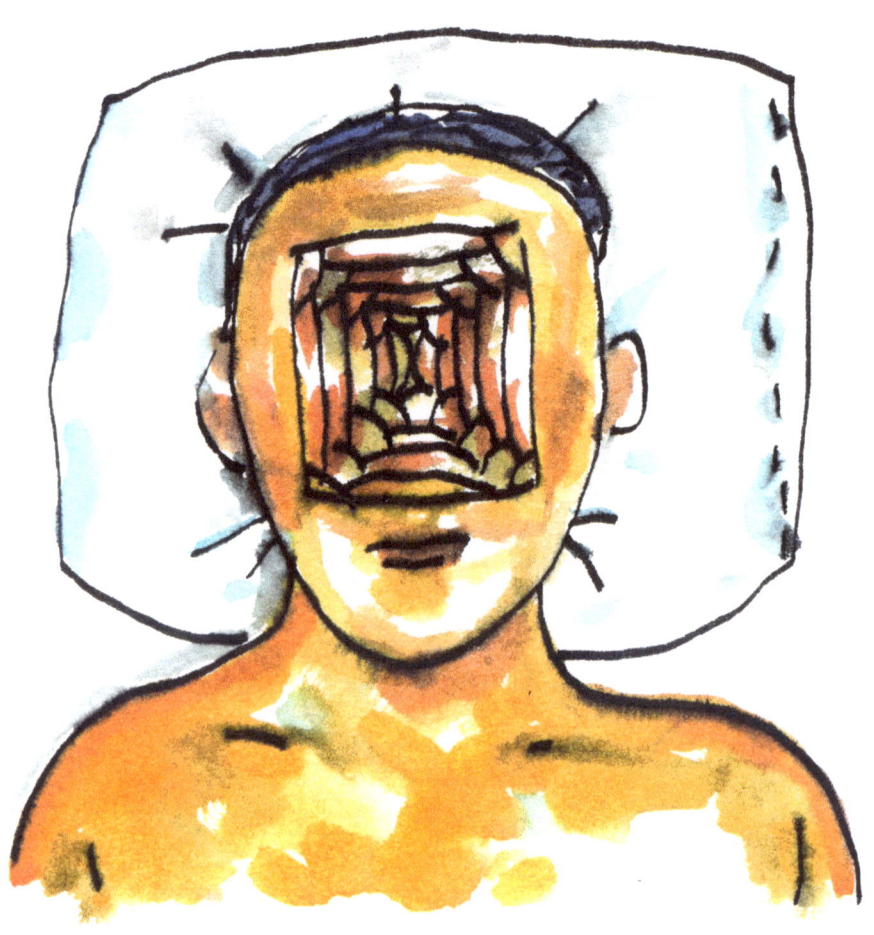

From now on, we'll put a guard on anyone who's sleeping.

SOFT SKIN INSIDE HIS MOUTH

Who's up there?

You're getting worried, aren't you, Alan?

The ocean is my province.

We need you. You can't afford the luxury of cracking up.

I'm not easy to get along with, am I.

From now on, we'll put a guard on anyone who's sleeping.

I looked right at them.

WE CAN'T TOUCH IT WHILE IT'S STILL UNDERWATER

Boatloads of fish had to be destroyed.

Perhaps these will be the bones we need to solve our problem.

I looked right at them.

Into the wastes of outer space. It's a fitting grave for an astronaut.

Nothing human would ever enter your mind.

Does frightening women make you proud?

THIS IS INTERVISION CALLING THE WORLD

Repeat. Condition desperate.

Do you want to hear the story or not?

Whatever you are, I came here to kill you.

Have I changed that much?

Fasten your seatbelts, gentlemen.

Does frightening women make you proud?

When I reached her she could only scream and whisper.

LIKE A DREAM IN THE NIGHT THEIR CIVILIZATION PERISHES

Something must've happened to Duke. He tried to kill me.

No, please. We mustn't speak of that ever.

When I reached her she could only scream and whisper.

They're bursting all around us.

Suggest continuing on to another galaxy.

Is it true that no one will ever really know what happened here?

I CAN'T GET THE ICEBERG OUT OF HIM!

There was a sort of humming noise.

I was far away. Unsuspecting. Unknown.

What kind of thing is down there?

It's as if some power were trying to tear us apart.

Listen, Tony. We're going to have to blast off right now.

Is it true that no one will ever really know what happened here?

You know, anything is possible.

**JOHNSON?
JOHNSON?
JOHNSON!**

You know there have been rumors.

You're making sounds but there's no message coming through.

You are not familiar with the focusing-disintegration ray?

You must not continue this monstrous slaughter.

You will not become the most powerful man on earth.

The next sacrifice takes place tomorrow.

The least you could do is ply me with liquor.

You know, anything is possible.

You speak in riddles. What is your name?

IT STARTED WITH AN ALL-OUT WAR BETWEEN THE SEXES

Well, it was dark. I couldn't swear to it.

It could've gone a dozen different ways.

You're all very quiet. Perhaps you're resigned to the inevitable.

I know where to get our men—human men.

Very well, but I wash my hands of all responsibility.

Believe me, I am not your slave.

You speak in riddles. What is your name?

The perfect place to hatch a brutal horror.

YOU HAVE BROUGHT DEATH UPON ALL IN THIS ROOM

It's a sunburst. Put on your helmets.

I'm pushing a button.

And this unknown enemy keeps on getting closer.

The perfect place to hatch a brutal horror.

All right, gentlemen, you all have your orders.

This is where either we die or it dies.

THIS IS WHERE EITHER WE DIE OR IT DIES

It was just a metal monster. Yet when its destruction was immanent it called my name.

Still sticking to your story about a mysterious creature?

It's dead. It's taken off. The controls have been set.

Sure is an eager beaver.

I know how touchy you enlisted men are.

A thing like this—it's too big to evaluate.

I'll take it from here, Bob.

HERE WE GO AGAIN

We have grown old and weak.

We are not as crazy as you might think.

We don't know what action they'll take.

We'll have to do an autopsy.

We weren't dreaming. These bodies really existed.

We're not interested in your primitive emotions. We're scientists.

We're being hurled into space.

We gotta do it because the whole world's at stake.

We've sighted a moving object underneath the water.

We better get out of here.

We don't know what action they'll take.

We come from a world called Zon.

We can transform all the continents and make a life of plenty for all mankind.

We have within our grasp the limitless clean heat of the inner earth.

I'll take it from here, Bob.

I'm ashamed to be alive.

THEY'VE CLASSIFIED THE SKY TOP SECRET NOW

Maybe we could use a helicopter.

We've certainly got enough bones to work with.

Foolish women—running like rabbits in the night.

You're either fools, or very brave men.

I'm ashamed to be alive.

Since you've been here last, I've been thinking deeply.

YOU'RE ASKING ME TO SABOTAGE THE ENTIRE WORLD

Aren't you afraid I'll murder you all in your sleep?

Since you've been here last, I've been thinking deeply.

That river enters into a gigantic, bottomless volcanic lake.

I feel like I'm suffering from some terrible disease—like I've got no blood in my veins.

Haven't you heard, I'm a mental case.

I heard everything that Teddy said and none of it made any sense.

If you wish, call it a premonition.

THE TRICKS THEY TRIED, HOW CHILDISH THEY WERE

Your wife and unborn child are starving.

Any further damage reports?

Most of them are victims of that burning acid slime.

You can read all about it in the papers tomorrow.

If you wish, call it a premonition.

It doesn't even resemble human skin anymore.

IF YOU WISH, CALL IT A PREMONITION

A policeman hears a lot of strange stories.

This is a true story. Only the facts have been completely distorted.

The world wants to know what happened. I will tell them.

It's gonna be hard to keep the lid on now.

It doesn't even resemble human skin anymore.

I shall be back tomorrow night. Bon soir.

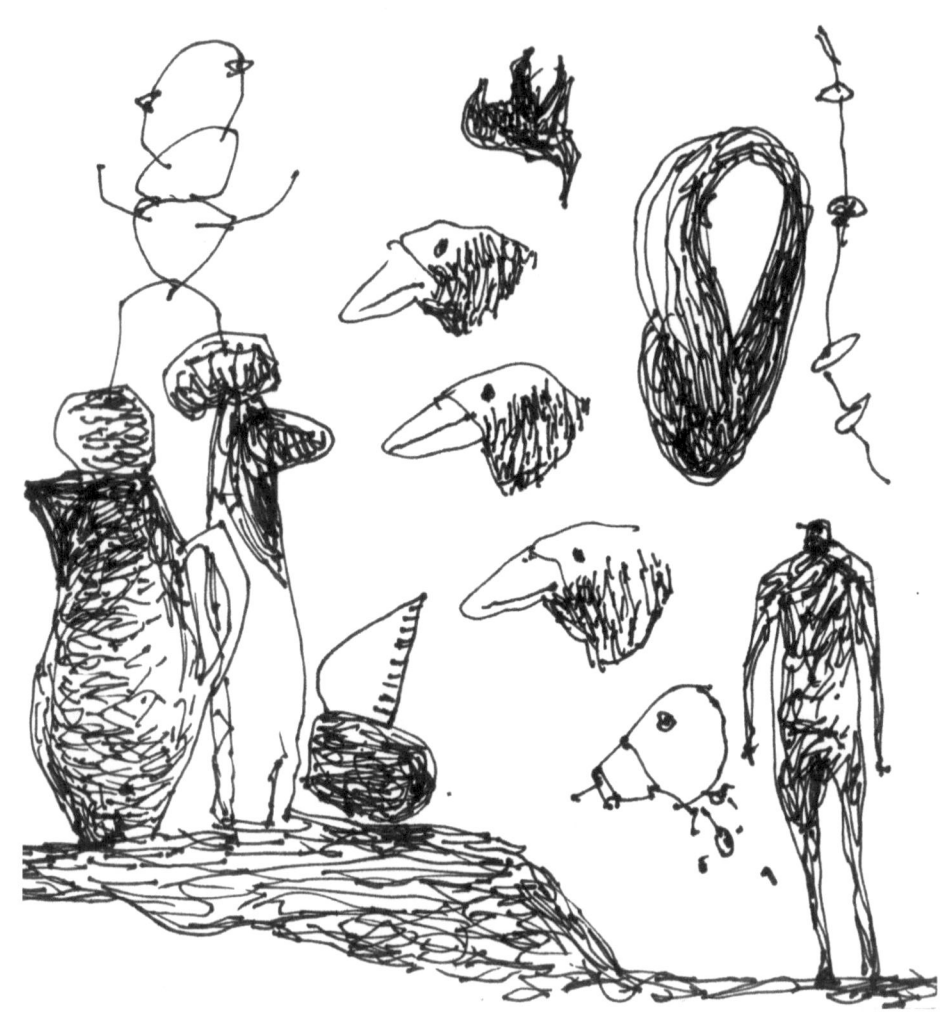

Her mind refuses to remember.

HER MIND REFUSES TO REMEMBER

The creatures of your planet are not ready for outer space.

Fantastic, incredible—I never really believed it.

Let's not try to figure it out now.

Track down this thing. Find out what it is, then destroy it.

But will you grow new legs when I have taken yours from you?

Maybe if I call to them they will answer—their ghosts will answer.

MAYBE IF I CALL TO THEM THEY WILL ANSWER—THEIR GHOSTS WILL ANSWER

You will bring the message to your people.

The area is going to be blown up with the entire colony of living dead.

We will die on a strange planet, in a strange galaxy.

This guy is six kinds of a freak.

If anyone asked me, I'd have to say it was the oxygen that killed him.

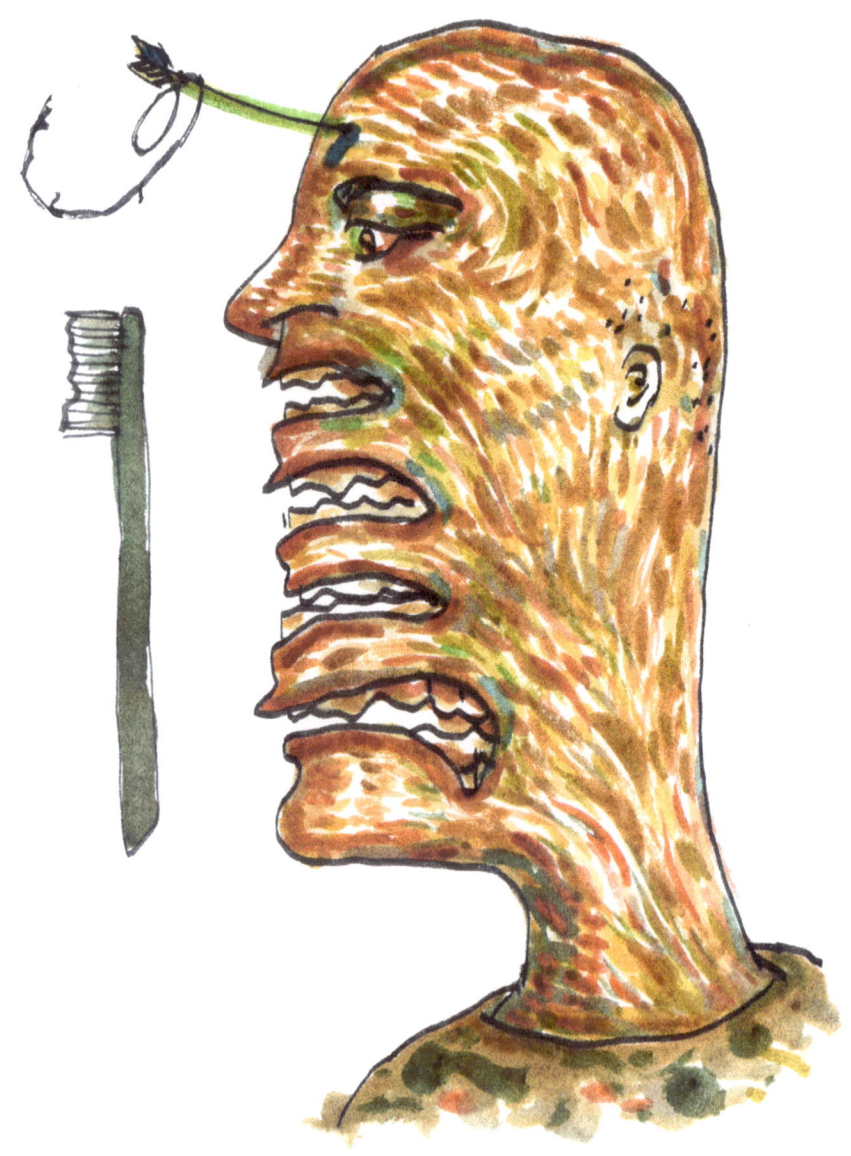

My eyes are alien. Look at them.

A SOOTHING OINTMENT?

Suddenly he screamed and ran from the room.

Maybe they're married or something.

My eyes are alien. Look at them.

And the radio is on the blink. So we can forget about the spaceman for the day.

You take away a man's mind and emotions and all you have is death—a living death.

Welcome back to the happy circle.

Wait a minute. Bombs don't unscrew.

WE WOULD GREET THEM AS EQUAL PARTNERS IN THE UNIVERSE

Wait a minute. Bombs don't unscrew.

Of course not. It's just part of my job.

Only their shadows remain.

That book has indeed made you forget so many things.

Good night, Robert.

Let's back out quietly.

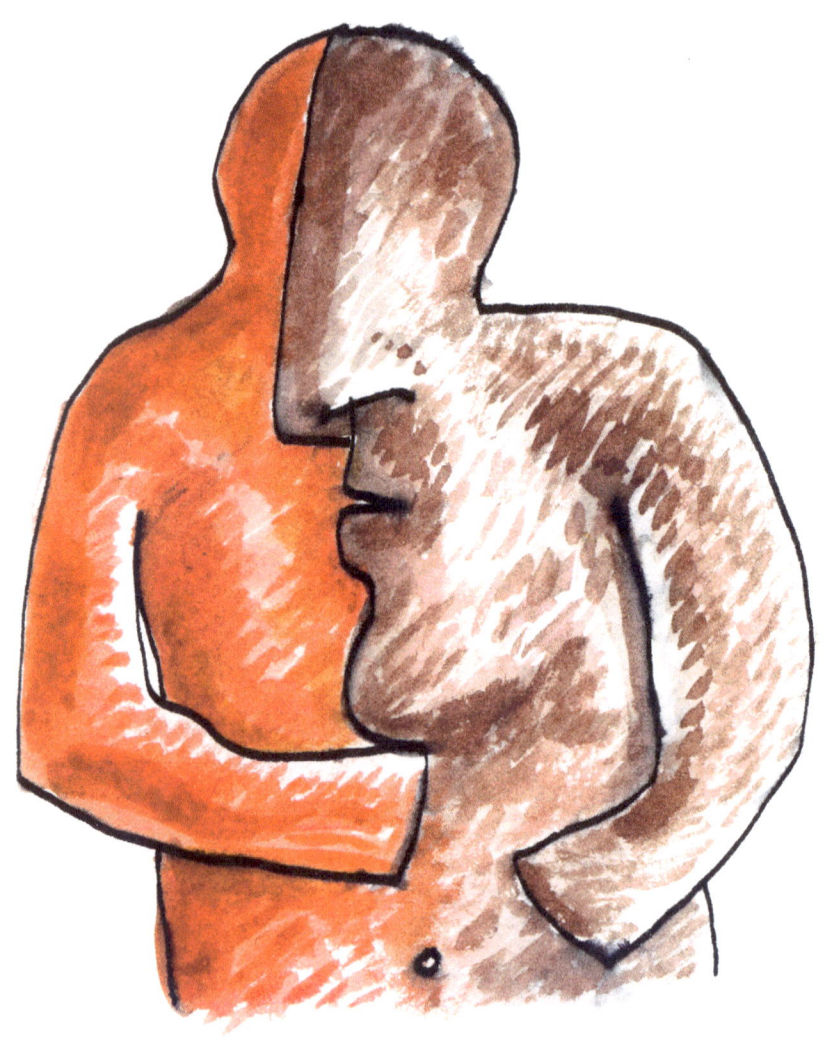

It's a good thing there are no more like him.

WHAT MAKES YOU THINK BETTY'S IN THE CELLAR?

Things of an alien source are appearing in the sky.

It was probably just a deer—these mountains are full of them.

Babies are bred and raised like livestock.

They have no right to put you in such danger.

That man has a badge instead of a brain.

It's a good thing there are no more like him.

Martinis? Two. Dry. Very dry.

NOTHING CAN RESIST THIS POWER

I merely tell you the future of your planet is at stake.
Tomorrow you'll be one of us.
How can you just stand there as if nothing were wrong?

Well, the whole thing is still a little hard to swallow.
I must say you don't look dangerous.
I merely tell you the future of your planet is at stake.

It started with the moon first.
Our hopes and aspirations led us to the stars.
How can you just stand there as if nothing were wrong?

I can see no other hope for your planet.
Do not be shocked that the weapon speaks.
I merely tell you the future of your planet is at stake.

That means that somebody around here was tampering with time.
Time is, indeed, the only element, Doctor.
How can you just stand there as if nothing were wrong?

Radio contact with earth is no longer possible.
Martinis? Two. Dry. Very dry.
I merely tell you the future of your planet is at stake.

I wonder what kind of world we're opening the door on.
I shall go there in one of your bodies.
I merely tell you the future of your planet is at stake.
How can you just stand there as if nothing were wrong.

Well, it was dark. I couldn't swear to it.

IT COULD BE OUR BABY

Alan, there's more to this than just Duke and those birds.

I don't want to hurt you, but there are times when I just have to trust my own judgment about things.

Well, it was dark. I couldn't swear to it.

Twin worlds surrounded by eternal night and perpetual cold.

THEY LOOKED LIKE DEAD FISH

Twin worlds surrounded by eternal night and perpetual cold.

Then somebody remembered.

We know it's not a dead planet—completely.

The thing is that all fires must one day burn out.

Next to that, I look dandy.

WHY IS IT ALWAYS SO COSTLY FOR MAN TO MOVE FROM THE PRESENT TO THE FUTURE?

There's something wrong here, Filbrick.

There's a tragic side to this history-making event.

Next to that, I look dandy.

I only care about the idea.

PUT THE GUN AWAY

You're just a stubborn guy.

It's taken this to prove it.

To throw imaginary problems at the ceiling.

I wore long underwear.

I only care about the idea.

We've got a 50-foot spider out there on the loose.

My beams are focused on your blasters, gentlemen.

WHERE WOULD BE SAFER THAN CITY HALL?

All observers prepare for the blinding flash of the bomb.

My beams are focused on your blasters, gentlemen.

I am here—the dream that possesses your soul.

You look like a man who just inherited a greater portion of the world.

I have no information of my own probability of life or death.

Her sweater was found somewhere in the woods.

It broke out of its cage and grabbed me by the arm.

If the man was dead, how could he have a memory?

NOTHING WAS EFFECTIVE AGAINST THEM

The rout of civilization, the end of humanity. It's been nonexistent for over a hundred years.

If the man was dead, how could he have a memory?

Who can tell when those particles will float down to earth again?

There are always ultra-conservative pressure groups set against advancement.

I'm gonna loosen this belt. It's uncomfortable.

I think she's covered in a thin, protective metal of some kind.

I KNOW, YOU WANT TO KNOW WHERE YOU ARE

You've mastered the intricacies of that system, have you?

I'll send down a net.

You know, I haven't seen any insect life since we arrived.

I'm going to check the fuel supply.

You see, the electricity's been neutralized all over the world.

I've partially deactivated your muscular system.

You're being taken to a rendezvous with fate.

I think she's covered in a thin, protective metal of some kind.

You men have all the fun.

I think we're jumping at shadows.

You don't know what killed those cows.

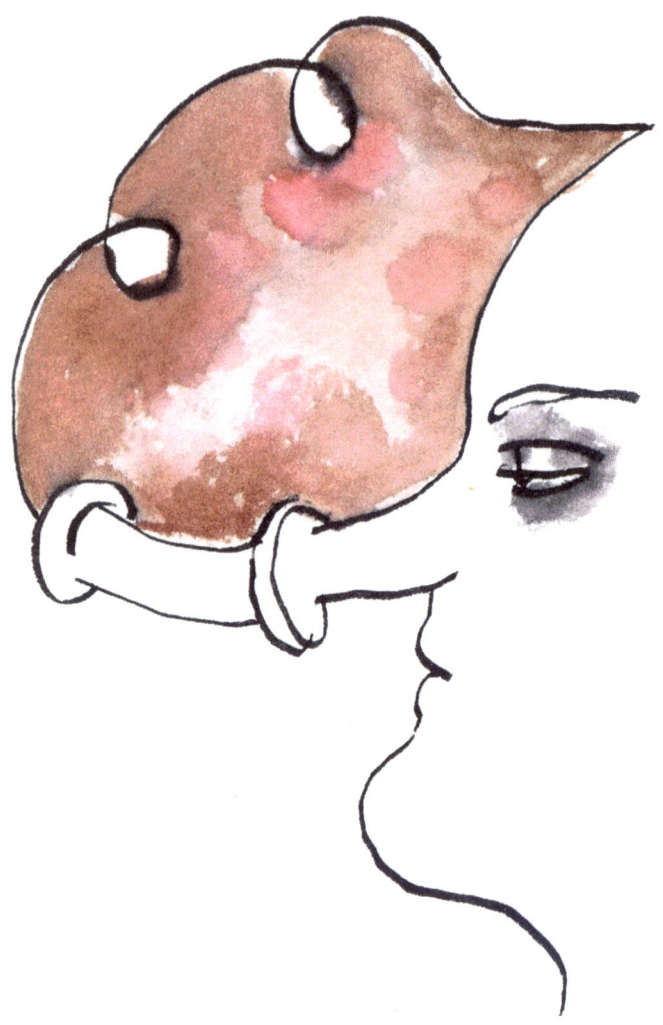

I'm hungry too.

TONIGHT FOR THE FIRST TIME IN HISTORY A ROBOT KILLED A MAN

Shouldn't you try to communicate with them first, and shoot them later if you have to?

Animals or humans, he just seems to like killing humans.

He could've been a fine soldier, but he got a sudden passion for astronomy.

And when you fire, aim directly at his heart.

I'm hungry too.

They found your husband dead in the wreckage.

ZONTAR IS ON ITS WAY, DARLING

Got to hit him right in the puss if you want to stop him, Colonel.

Look Kearn—volcanic bone-like metal—a good source of oxygen.

If this is Vargas' grave, where are his bones?

I sent them back to Shiloh.

Take a couple of divers and go after Johnson's body in the morning.

Indian Joe, what's he got to do with it?

Looks like a typical haunted house, doesn't it, Jim?

Start blasting it, Bob.

Not now, Connie. Stay out of this.

They found your husband dead in the wreckage.

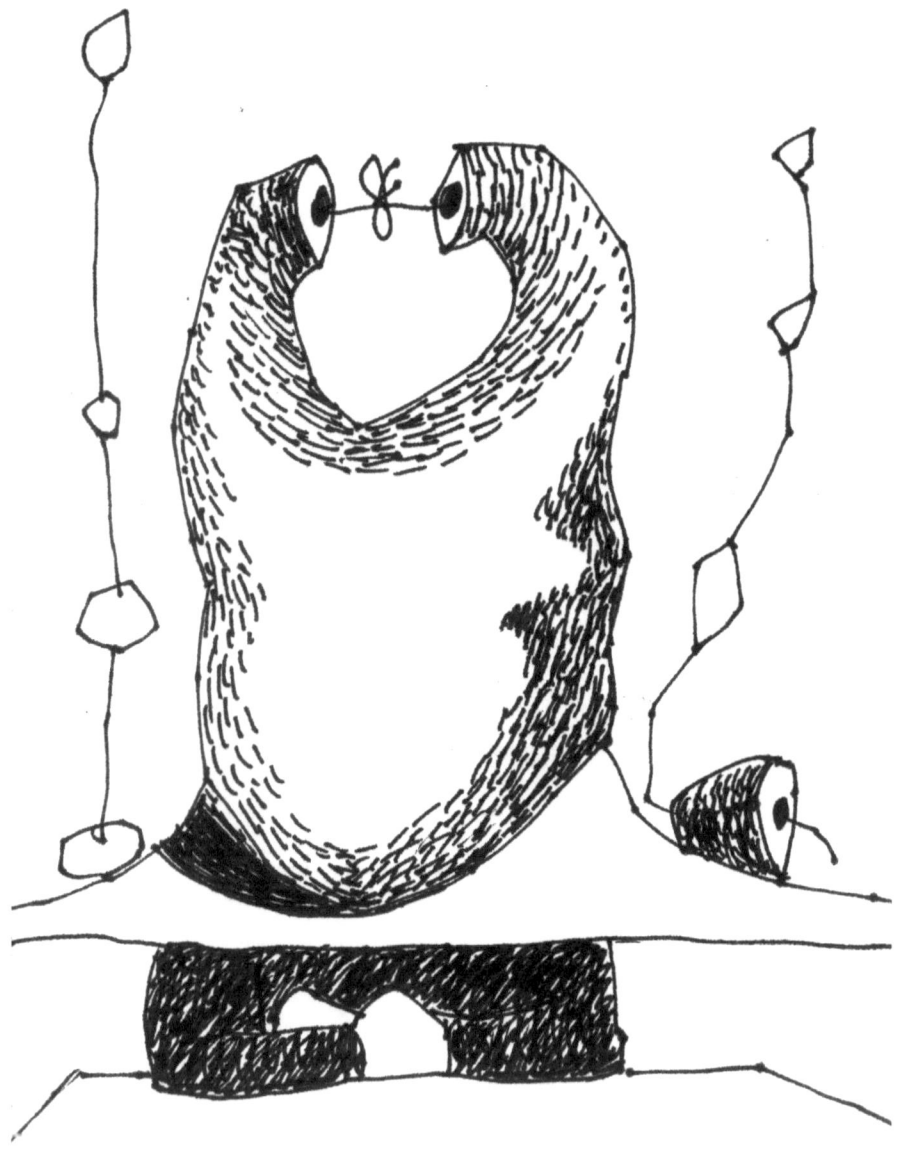

He's after me, not you.

AFTER THAT THEY STARTED ACTING STRANGELY

I don't know about the unconscious of the body you take over, but as far as I'm concerned, there's nothing childish about it.

I mean, it's blurred and twisted.

The creatures have taken over his body.

You talk as if this thing were a personal friend of yours.

He's my favorite astronomer.

He's after me, not you.

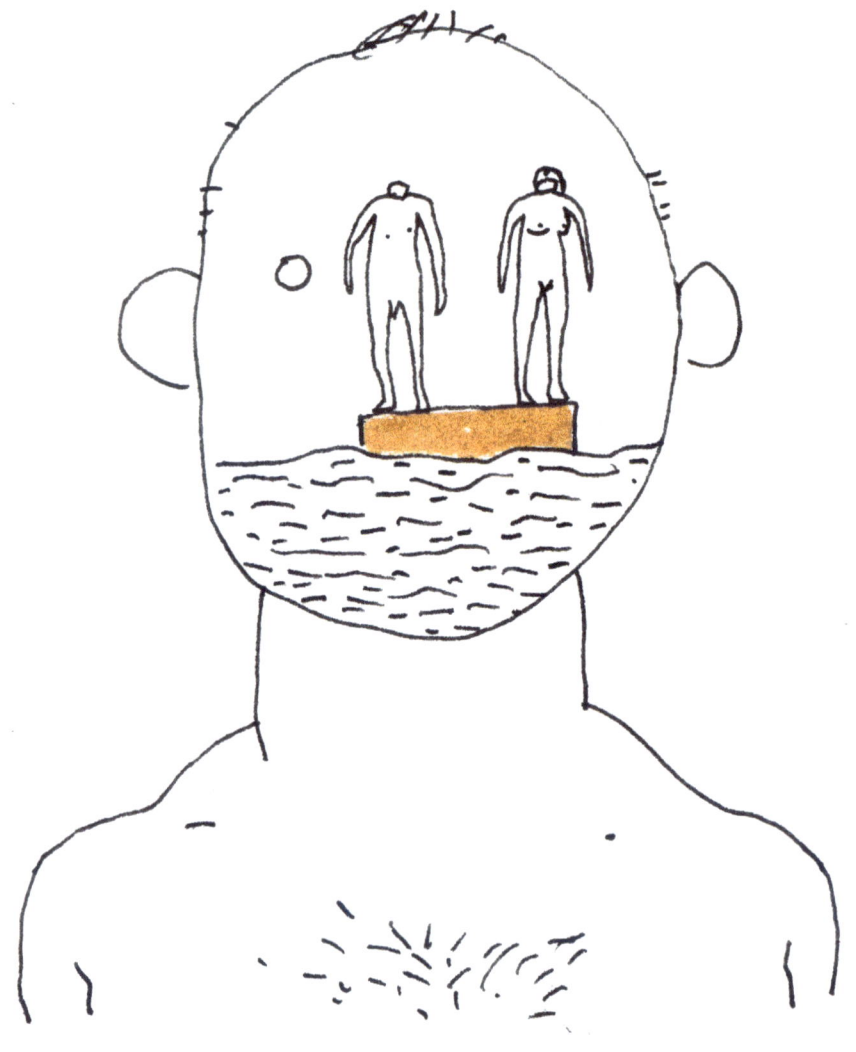

We're in a headlong race toward disappearance.

REMEMBER WHAT YOU LEARNED HERE TODAY

What do you do—change brains?

Yes it's true, I am your only friend.

Can't you understand they don't want you around for your own good.

And while we're waiting here for your miracle . . .

We're in a headlong race toward disappearance.

My circuits are unoffended.

IT MUST BE A TERRIBLE THING TO BE SO AFRAID

The scent had stopped right in the middle of nowhere.

You're being panicked by one incident.

You're going to stick around here and end up like Brad did.

And nobody can tell why these fish are dead.

Man is unfit as yet to receive this knowledge.

My circuits are unoffended.

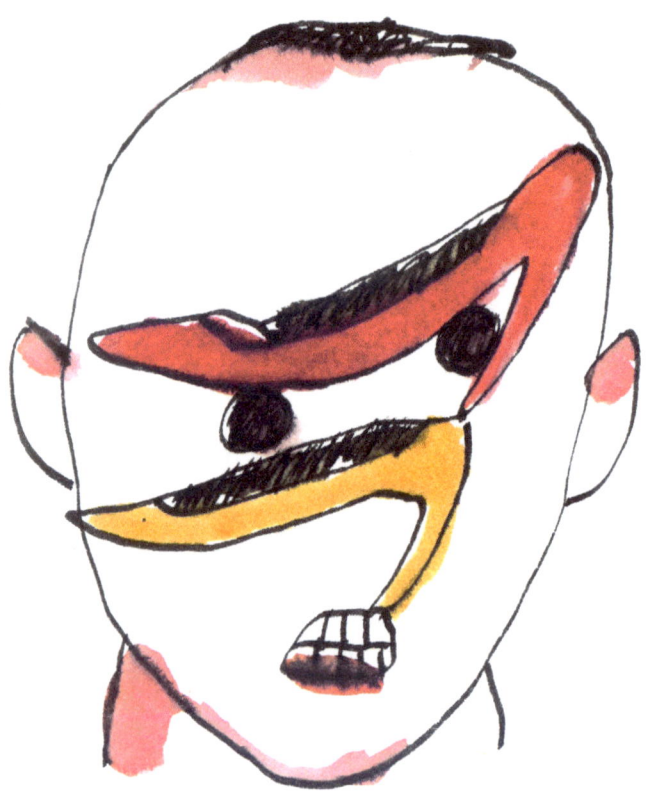

Look at those shoes. They're a mess.

SOMETHING WENT WRONG, IT'S AS SIMPLE AS THAT

Look at those shoes. They're a mess.

And no more hamburgers.

Since when must I tell you how to find a man?

You will never see your world again.

Can't we go on foot?

We're going to pay that mirage a little visit.

HIS MIND DOESN'T WANT TO REMEMBER THE DETAILS

To himself, every man is a whole world.

There's no need for love.

I'm always fearful when I see people exchange fear for reason.

Whatever he says, pretend you agree with him.

We're going to pay that mirage a little visit.

Everything seems *all right.*

EVERYTHING *SEEMS* ALL RIGHT

There was happiness. There was love.

You were dead.

Something terrible.

You were a fool, Derrick.

There'll be other moonlight nights.

And what about the others?

I'm sorry, sir. I'm not taking orders anymore.

The earth won't hear us.

Never fails to fascinate me from up here.

ALPHA 2 DOES NOT ANSWER

How do I give that signal meaning?

Everybody wonders. They just don't like to talk about it.

Never fails to fascinate me from up here.

Shark is God.

I PRESENT YOU WITH THE POSSIBILITY OF SAVING THE HUMAN RACE

I have been groping my way through a maze of fear and doubt.

Like a blade goes through mercury.

As if somebody just plucked him out of a dish like candy.

We might as well pick up what's left.

As soon as I fix my regulator.

Shark is God.

And I thought those people were seeing things.

WE CAN'T HAND OUT BLOOD LIKE GASOLINE

We're friends. We welcome you.

We do not pretend to have achieved perfection.

I bet they don't show.

I must confess I'm completely baffled.

It sounded like "Lockhart."

And I thought those people were seeing things.

Does anything really matter to you anymore?

That's what we have to find out before they kill us all.

Well I guess that's all, and thank you for your patience.

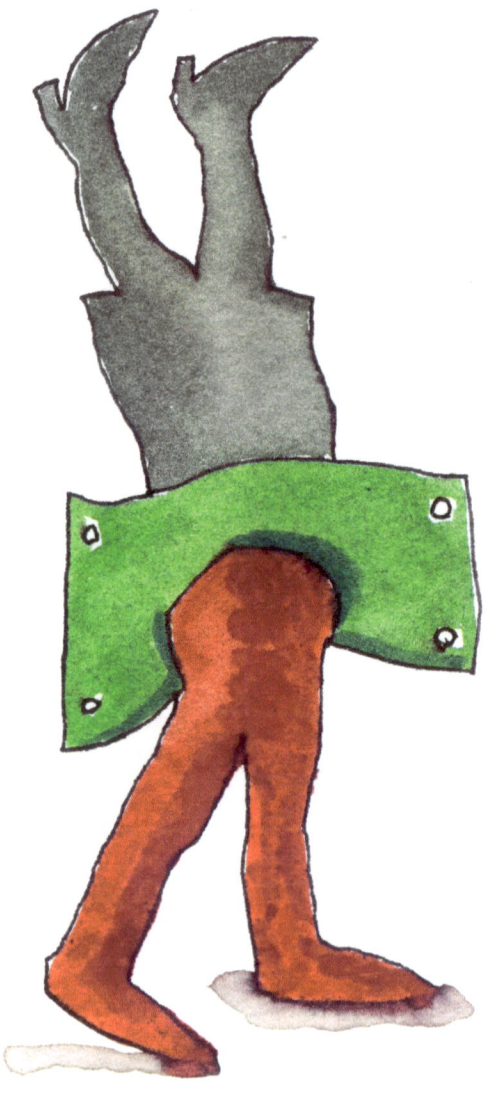

Come on, Janet. We don't want to miss any part of that double feature.

CODA

Could you possibly send someone else?

SCI FI MOVIES

A Giant Claw (1957)
Assignment: Outer Space (1960)
Atragon (1963)
Attack of the Crab Monsters (1957)
Battle in Outer Space (1959)
Battle of the Satellites (1958)
Battle of the Worlds (1961)
Crack in the World (1964)
Destination Moon (1950)
Devil Girl from Mars (1954)
Earth Versus the Flying Saucers (1956)
First Man into Space (1958)
First Spaceship on Venus (1962)
Flight to Mars (1951)
Forbidden Planet (1956)
Giant Behemoth (1959)
Giant from the Unknown (1958)
I Married a Monster from Outer Space (1958)
Invaders from Mars (1953)
Invasion of the Body Snatchers (1955)
Invasion of the Star Creatures (1962)
Invisible of Invaders (1959)
It! The Terror from Beyond Space (1958)
Journey to the Seventh Planet (1962)
Killers from Space (1954)
Mars Needs Women (1966)
Not of This Earth (1957)
Queen of Blood (1966)
Queen of Outer Space (1958)
Phantom from Space (1953)
Planet of the Vampires (1965)
Project Moon Base (1963)
Radar Men from the Moon (1952)
Red Planet Mars (1952)
Reptilicus (1961)
Robinson Crusoe on Mars (1964)
Rocketship X-M (1950)
She Gods of Shark Reef (1958)
Stranger from Venus (1954)
Target Earth (1954)
Teenagers from Outer Space (1959)
The Angry Red Planet (1959)
The Atomic Submarine (1959)
The Astounding She-Monster (1958)
The Beast with a Million Eyes (1955)
The Brain from Planet Arous (1958)
The Creation of the Humanoids (1962)
The Day the Earth Stood Still (1951)
The Man from Planet X (1951)
The Monster that Challenged the World (1957)
The Phantom Planet (1961)
The Yesterday Machine (1963)
Them! (1954)
They Came from Beyond Space (1967)
This Island Earth (1954)
20 Million Miles to Earth (1957)
War Between the Planets (1966)
War of the Worlds (1953)
Warning from Space (1956)
X – The Unknown (1956)
Zontar: The Thing from Venus (1966)

ACKNOWLEDGEMENTS

The following poems have appeared in literary journals:

"Once my air is out, water won't matter," "Every woman in the world, we all live in fear," "Making a decision like that would scare anyone," "There's not a drop of booze left in this house," "A spaceship from where? From outer space," and "Who am I to stand in the way of science" in *The Offending Adam*

"Power, power you can't conceive," "They've classified the sky top secret now," "The tricks they tried, how childish they were," and "If you wish, call it a premonition" in *Mental Shoes*

What Books gratefully acknowledges the support of AVK ARTS FOUNDATION for its assistance in publishing this book.

CHUCK ROSENTHAL is the author of a memoir, two books of Magic Journalism, and nine novels, including the sci-fi detective novel *The Heart of Mars*. He lives in Topanga Canyon, home to many UFO sightings, and is a member of The Glass Table Collective.

GAIL WRONSKY, a poet, essayist, and translator, is the author of ten books, including *So Quick Bright Things* and *Poems for Infidels*. She, too, lives in Topanga Canyon and is a member of the Glass Table Collective.

GRONK is a Chicano painter, print maker, and performance artist known for his murals and stage design. He has exhibited at many museums including the Los Angeles County Museum of Art, the Corcoran Gallery in Washington, D.C., and the M. H. de Young Memorial Museum in San Francisco. A founding member of ASCO, a multi-media arts collective, Gronk lives in downtown Los Angeles and is a member of the Glass Table Collective. His book of drawings, *A Giant Claw*, was published by What Books Press.

TITLES FROM
WHAT BOOKS PRESS

POETRY
Molly Bendall & Gail Wronsky, *Bling & Fringe (The L.A. Poems)*
Kevin Cantwell, *One of Those Russian Novels*
Ramón García, *Other Countries*
Karen Kevorkian, *Lizard Dream*
Chuck Rosenthal, Gail Wronsky, Gronk, *Tomorrow You'll Be One of Us: Sci Fi Poems*
Judith Taylor, *Sex Libris*
Lynne Thompson, *Start with a Small Guitar*
Gail Wronsky, *So Quick Bright Things*, bilingual, Spanish, tr. Alicia Partnoy

FICTION
François Camoin, *April, May, and So On*
A.W. DeAnnuntis, *Master Siger's Dream*
A.W. DeAnnuntis, *The Mermaid at the Americana Arms Motel*
Katharine Haake, *The Origin of Stars and Other Stories*
Katharine Haake, *The Time of Quarantine*
Mona Houghton, *Frottage & Even As We Speak: Two Novellas*
Rod Val Moore, *Brittle Star*
Chuck Rosenthal, *Coyote O'Donohughe's History of Texas*

MAGIC JOURNALISM
Chuck Rosenthal, *Are We Not There Yet? Travels in Nepal, North India, and Bhutan*
Chuck Rosenthal, *West of Eden: A Life in 21st Century Los Angeles*

ART
Gronk, *A Giant Claw,* bilingual intro, Spanish
Chuck Rosenthal, Gail Wronsky, Gronk, *Tomorrow You'll Be One of Us: Sci Fi Poems*

LOS ANGELES

What Books Press books may be ordered from:
SPDBOOKS.ORG | ORDERS@SPDBOOKS.ORG | (800) 869 7553 | AMAZON.COM

Visit our website at
WHATBOOKSPRESS.COM

www.ingramcontent.com/pod-product-compliance
Lightning Source LLC
Chambersburg PA
CBHW041402160426
42811CB00109B/1959/J